Congratulations, Mama! What you have just done is truly a miracle. A little human grew inside of you. Now that beautiful baby is snuggled up warmly against your chest. You endured morning sickness, swollen ankles, intense cravings for strange foods, and walking—or rather waddling—around looking like a sleep-deprived penguin, and then (as if that wasn't difficult enough) you gave birth! Wow, you have done a lot.

Each one of these affirmations is taken from a specific moment I can remember when I was exactly where you are today. There were moments I was exhausted from waking up every few hours, and I needed to remember that there will be a day when I will sleep through the night again. There were moments I felt like an imposter, that I could never actually be a good mom, and I needed to remember that all good moms have doubts. My hope for this book is that you will get the encouragement you need to press on even when things are tough. Each day read one affirmation and take a moment to repeat it out loud to yourself. There is power in your words. Repeating these out loud and internalizing them will help you build the confidence you need to be that amazing mom that is already inside of you.

Be encouraged, Mama! All that you have done to get you this far should prove to yourself that you have great strength within you! Your new baby is a precious blessing that you get to enjoy. Are there difficult times? Yes. But don't forget that motherhood is a wonderful journey that is well worth it all. You have much to look forward to. Your future is bright.
Enjoy the journey!

I GREW A PERSON INSIDE OF ME.

I can do anything.

I will ask for help
when I need it

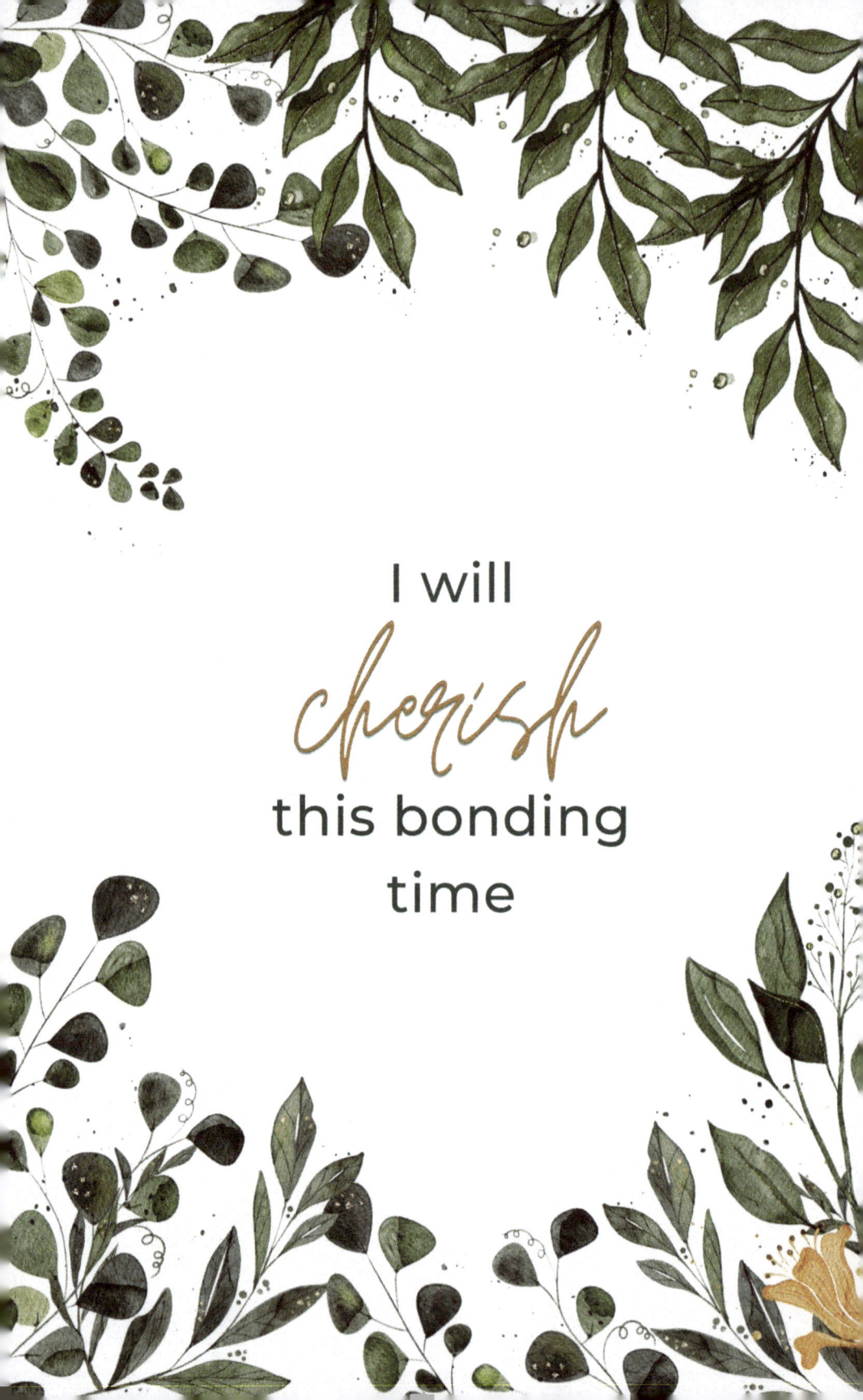

I will

cherish

this bonding
time

I will be

calm in

the chaos

MY VALUE IS NOT BASED ON HOW PRODUCTIVE I AM

Cherishing
time with
my new
baby is

*more
important*

than a
clean
house

I HAVE WHAT IT
TAKES TO BE A
GOOD MOM

I'm doing my best and that is enough

My journey is
my own.
I won't compare
myself to others.

I LET GO OF
PAST MISTAKES
AND LOOK TO
THE FUTURE
WITH HOPE

I will take
the day
one
moment at
a time

I will
CELEBRATE
the little
victories

I breathe out my
anxieties

**AND BREATHE
IN PEACE**

BABY AND I HAVE BEEN
THROUGH A LOT.
WE WILL RECOVER
together

I AM A

good

mom

Having fears and doubts does not make me a bad mom

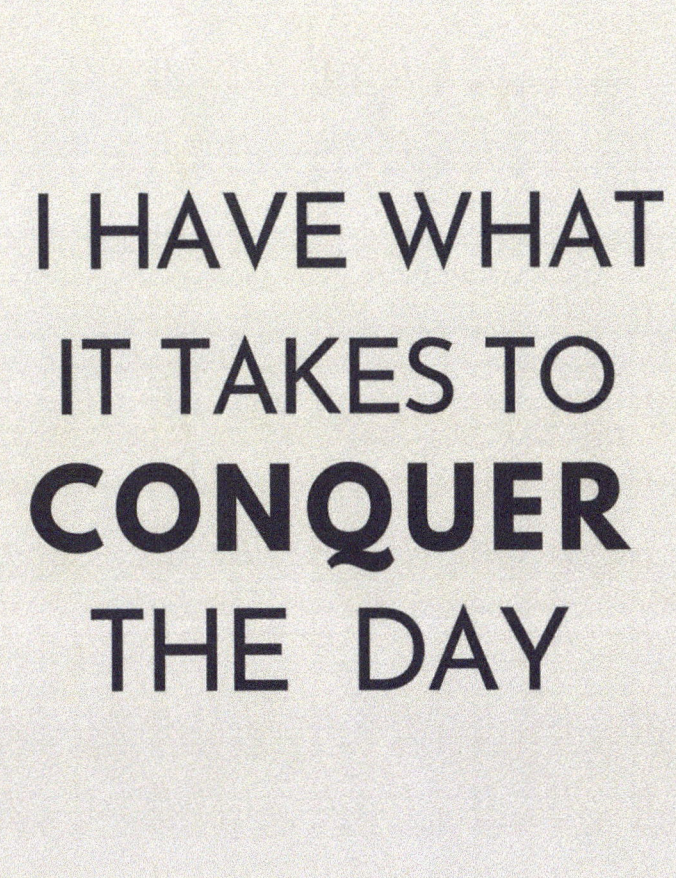

I HAVE WHAT IT TAKES TO **CONQUER** THE DAY

IT'S OK

to cry

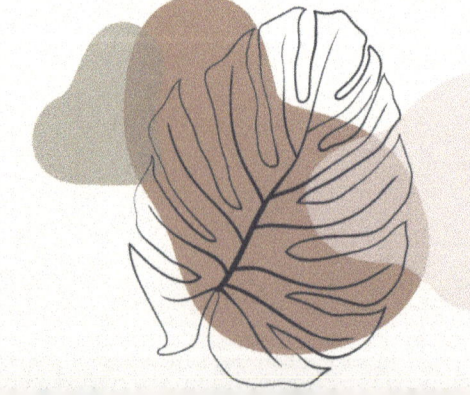

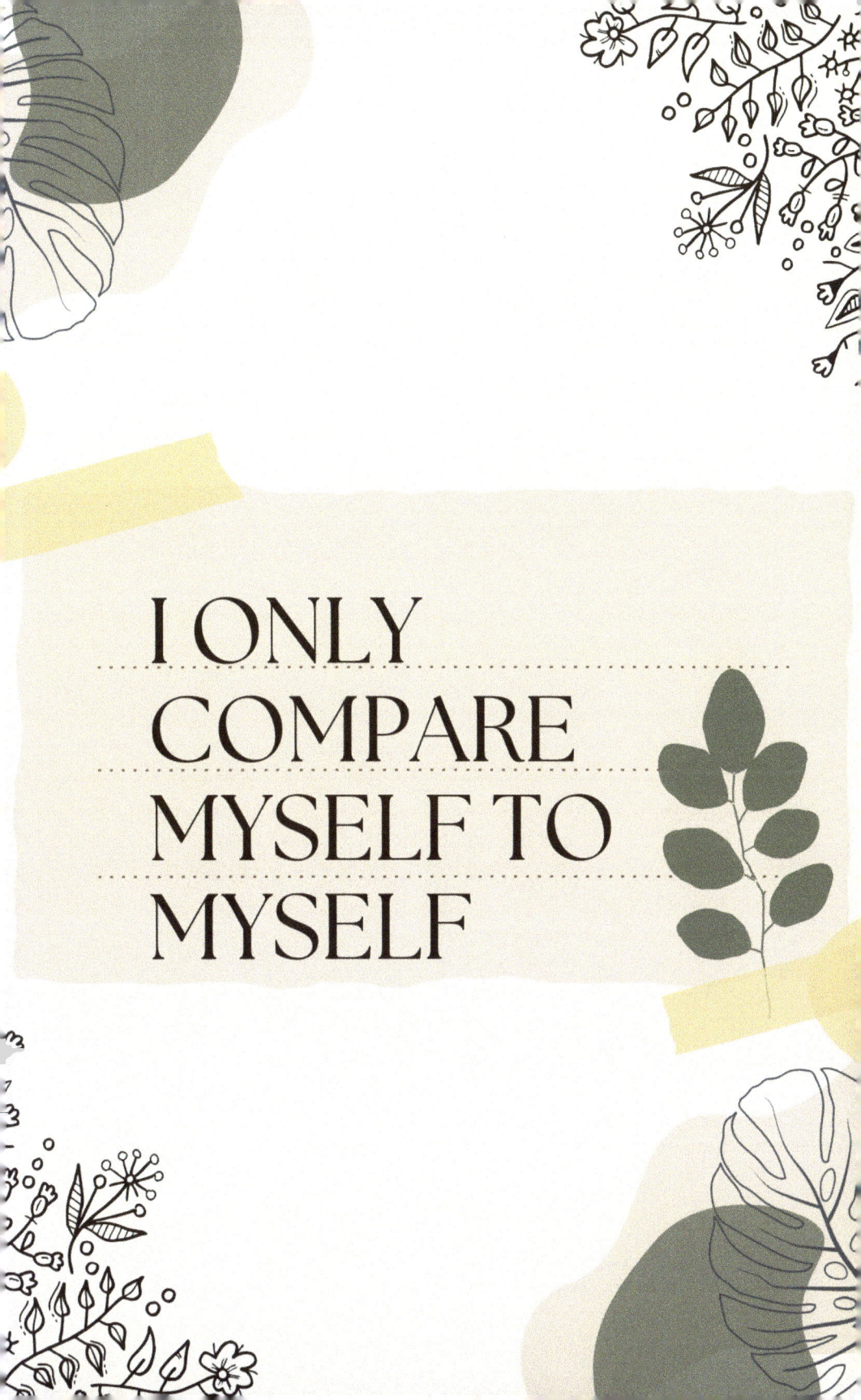

I ONLY COMPARE MYSELF TO MYSELF

I choose to be happy

I WILL

be kind

TO MYSELF

BEING A

MOM

HAS SHOWN ME I AM

STRONGER

THAN I KNEW

I choose
to stay
calm

All good moms have fears and frustrations

I WILL BE
PATIENT
WITH MY BODY
AND GIVE IT
TIME TO HEAL

I do not hold myself to the standard of perfection

The mess
can wait.
I will
rest.

I become a

better mom

every day

The time I spend

with my baby

is valuable

All good moms need a
break from time
to time.

"—

I am patient
with my baby
and patient
with myself

—"

I deserve to enjoy the precious moments of the newborn phase

No one is a perfect mom. But I will be a very good one.

I release
all
feelings
of
inadequacy

I'm grateful for this new chapter in my life.

I am
STRONG

I CAN DO

what needs to be done

I will cherish
the sweet moments in
every day

I'm a

Mom.

I can do

anything.

www.ingramcontent.com/pod-product-compliance
Lightning Source LLC
Chambersburg PA
CBHW051600120626
46551CB00013B/1602